ART *from the* ASHES

Columbia Artists Respond to the Sesquicentennial of the Burning of Their City

Edited by Cynthia Boiter

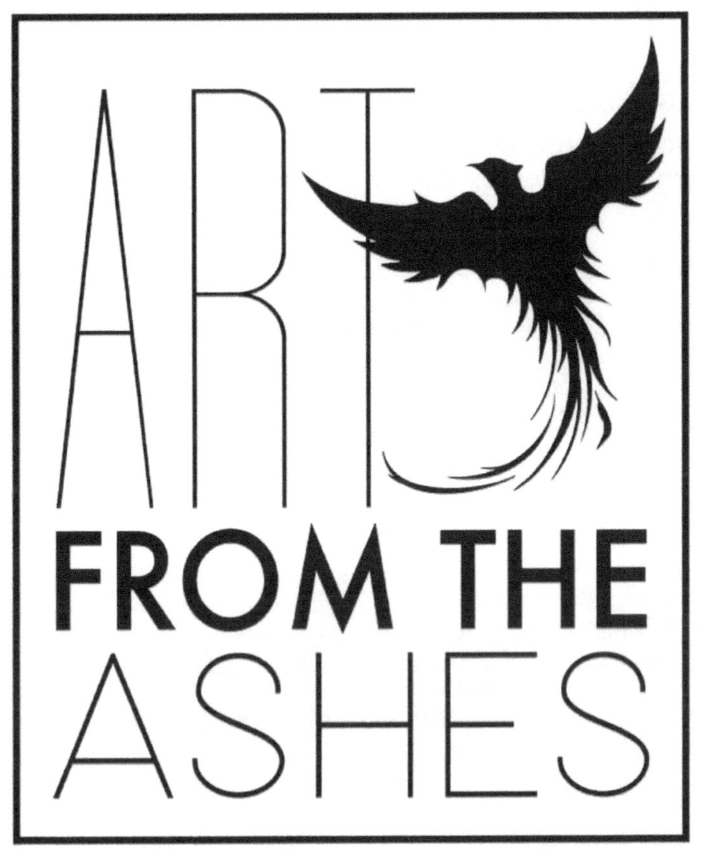

A Jasper Magazine Project

Edited by Cynthia Boiter

Muddy Ford Press, 1009 Muddy Ford Road, Chapin, SC 29036

Library of Congress Number 2015900512

ISBN 978-1-942081-01-2

Cover Art by Susan Lenz

Contents

INTRODUCTION

PYROLYSIS

By Cynthia Boiter

Does smoke from a fire ever fully clear the air? Or does it leave a film over the land that only seems to disappear, like a walking stick bug on a branch, as our eyes adjust to the remaining haze? A type of pollution to which we become accustomed.

Similarly, are there enough scented soaps or essential oils to rid the hair and skin of the trace of fire that lingers so intimately there before it blends with residual odors—of sweat and supper, sweet blood passed and born and spilt, turned earth, rain—and, on a molecular level, it becomes something neither new nor entirely different, but vaguely reminiscent of the remnants of nitrogen released ages ago?

How long until the soil exhausts the potassium and phosphorus that leeched from the ashes of a flame that smoldered for decades before it went ablaze?

These are the kinds of questions more than two dozen Columbia, South Carolina artists—visual, literary, and musical—asked themselves when they reflected on the sesquicentennial of the burning of their city.

There were no pro or con sides. No one scored points. The sidelines from which to cheer disappeared long ago into second growth pine and hardwood forests, fragile river banks, concrete, and a collective consciousness as vulnerable as a bruised shin. This group of enlightened creatives ventured into the question of where we are now and how we got to these disparate places on pins and needles with the bursts of cannons afire echoing in their ears. They spent time by the docks smelling the souring cotton then catching the caustic scent of smoldering cellulose. They stood there, invisible, and felt the heat of the flames that parched their skin, squinting their eyes against the intensity of the light, hoping for clarity, finding mostly only shadows—some at play, others still at war.

The invasion and burning of Columbia on February 17th, 1865 resulted in what might have been a complete paradigm shift for the residents and natives of South Carolina's state capital. It is a uniquely Southern trick that it did not. Consequently, the writers whose work is recorded within these pages, as well as the visual and musical artists who responded to the same call for clarity, offer few definitive answers to the questions of where we are now and how we have or have not recovered or reconstructed since the night the fires raged. In so many ways, we're still waiting for the smoke to clear.

HANDFUL OF NAILS, PART 1
THE UNDERTAKER

By Al Black

Before
this war of hubris
I was
a cabinet maker

crafter of tables & chairs
couches for the parlor
pie closets, shelves
dressers and beds
to lie on

Now

I hammer together
rough boards and nails
housing
for the dead

if the resurrection
comes to pass
a handful of nails
is all
they'll find

PART II
NATIVE SON

I was your native son
your barefoot soldier
your collateral damage

tenant farmer's son
forced to fight
or find other fields to plow

you planted me
along the hedgerow
no place for momma to pray
only a handful of nails
remain to testify
that once I was a man

PART III
SOLDIER BLUE

Soldier blue
Yankee Doodle Dandy
marched south then east
and north to heart of sedition

I saw America
not in Leaves of Grass
but in the blisters
on the soles of my feet

in Pee Dee gator swamps
typhoid found me
name and address
pinned upon my chest

my family will send
the undertaker
to build me a pine bed
with a handful of nails

and carry me north
so I don't have to
sleep alone in
blood red clay

THE CURIOUS

By Elizabeth Breen

"The raging fire was [an] invitation to stragglers, sightseers, and the curious that all such calamities attract." – Marion B. Lucas, *Sherman and the Burning of Columbia*

I want to see the fire but I've spent my life
in flames. My mouth is ash and my hair is gone.
I stir my coffee with a melted spoon.

I want to see the fire but my windows are
rippled from heat. The curtains are black
I've got closets of wire hangers. The neighbor

scrapes his matches against my bones.
It is winter again, he says. My floorboards
are black and the roof is gone. The sky

is a calamity. There's smoke coming
from the city; the dog is running into town.
I want to see the fire but I've burned

it all before. From here, the city
is incandescent. There's heat
all around and I am radiant.

FEBRUARY WEATHER

By Jonathan Butler

History tells us little about the weather.
How, for example, the morning after the fires,
a light drizzle fell on the fallen city,
and the wind smelled of ash among the ruins.

Even less do historians note the grass
jutting out from under the scorched lawn's rubble,
or whether the silence of deserted streets
was broken by a crow's call overhead.

And history books say nothing of the weight
of papers folded into an overcoat pocket
of someone approaching beneath a black umbrella
delivering tidings of war or letters of love

whose authors, perhaps, are already among the dead.

A SIMPLE EXPLANATION

Debra A. Daniel

Start with a boy, skin black as charred wood. See him flee.
Begin with that spark, a flicker careening through the leap
of fierce heat, through the billowing stench, the acrid
shriek.
See the gash of his teeth, his mouth pinched in a crease
that cinches his keening, that seizes his scream.

Add the scrape of a woman crouched in the street, her
face
pale as cotton, her hair singed and dingy, her wilted dis-
may.
Add her dragging a mattress, tattered and frayed
down stairs, cross the porch toward the fractured sway
of chests and chairs, the mush of ash and mud, soggy and
gray.

Shift to the captured soldier, starving, sick, too weak to
stand
when the others ran. Stay with him through the night
stranded
in the barren field, no tent, no blanket to block the batter-
ing path
of wind, the frigid winter damp. See his eyes lift and scan

the glaring sky. Feel the fevered glow. Feel the flare of wrath.

Imagine the brothel's red lights. Smell the thick smoke in the parlor.
Pick the harlot with a thirsty itch for whiskey, its prickly scorch,
her scalding need for each bitter swallow. Watch as she arches
the low of her back, barters her pelvis and breasts as a force
to coerce Yankee men to lay down their torches.

Walk through the ruined streets, through the lost and the saved,
past the powerful men, past the ladies of grace,
through the hustlers, the whores, the soldiers, the slaves.
Smell the rot. Hear the moans. Feel them curse. Watch them pray.
Sift through ashes and cinders, through anger and hate.

Surely they suffered. Surely they mourned.
They believed so profoundly that they started a war.
So what can be salvaged from the sooty debris
as we dig through their relics to make sense of their grief?
Shall we start with that black boy? End with him. Set him free.

MY HEROES HAD NEVER BEEN YANKEES

Told from the viewpoint of a Southerner; borrowed from the viewpoint of Sherman Alexie (The only other Sherman that I know of)

By William Garland

1.

In the textbooks of my younger days we learned that it was best to spit on the name of General William Tecumseh Sherman. On November 15, 1864, the man marched down to the sea in Georgia and then he kicked off the New Year by marching back up through the Carolinas, just to burn everything he and his boys could get their hands on. We were always shown the same picture, and we always knew that the man had never figured out how to crack a smile. *Old times, they are not forgotten.*

2.

In Columbia, we're told that Sherman had it out for us. The whole thing started in the First Baptist Church and that never sat too well with the Union Army. They told us those Yankees burned the city to the ground. And the tales of destruction grew every time they told us about it. *Sherman never shed a tear over the burning.*

3.

Did you know that the scene in *Gone with the Wind* that we all know as "the Burning of Atlanta" was not actually referring to that time when Sherman burned the city, but the time when the city was torched two months earlier, when the Confederates torched their ammunition dumps to keep the Yankees from stealing them when they marched into town? I've also been told that Gerald O'Hara's horse in the movie was later promoted to Silver in *The Lone Ranger*.

4.

I was thirteen years old when I walked away from a campfire that took out an acre. I hid in my mother's bathtub and the sirens wailed by outside. Neighbors stepped on their stoops and shook hands while they watched my fire grow. The smoke was the thing that lasted, at least that's the thing that I remembered. Folks say it rolls, but that's not quite it. Smoke covers you. It saturates the air and clogs up your skin to the point where you understand that skin actually does breathe.

5.

Look a-way! Look a-way! Look a-way! Dixie Land. Sherman is a coming and he's gonna burn all that he can.

6.

My first job in Columbia was at Washington Street Methodist Church. The burning of the old church building wasn't the first thing they told me about, but it didn't take a full month for me to hear that it had been torched on account of a janitor over at the First Baptist Church across the street. The story was that he'd convinced a handful of soldiers that the First Baptist Church was actually our church. It's all hearsay, but I was handed a copy of the book that told the story anyway.

6A.

The events leading up to the burning of the church we only know by hearsay... J.F. Williams, who was a boy of fifteen in 1865, recalled that Bell, a young black, had told him several times what had happened... "A Troop of northern soldiers came to the church and asked if it were the First Baptist Church."... The sexton of the church told them "it was not but that the First Baptist Church was just around the corner and pointed it out to them." And then "a short time later Washington Street Methodist Church was in flames." This was the rumor and the generally accepted theory.

6B.

You don't have to live in Columbia long (or any other city that has the distinction of being on the path of Sherman's

March) to hear all kinds of stories about that son-of-a-bitch who burnt down the family estate, or the family church, or the family business, or even the family treasure. *It's this badge of honor for some Southerners to have an ancestor whose house was burned by Sherman's troops.* I'd heard stories of a lady that had to fight off Sherman's men with a broom three different times only to have the house torched on their fourth try. In fact, the only thing that holds more weight is to have a story about how your ancestors had managed to save the estate by guile or by firing the family silver at them from a cannon that you just happened to have on the property. But for the most part, you're just going to hear about things burning.

7.

Driving to the beach with my folks when I was a little boy, I asked them what God looked like. The Man they pieced together sounds like He could be General Lee's long, lost brother.

8.

It's the same old story that we heard time-and-time again: There was an accidental fire that broke out in the red light district, the Union boys got liquored up on the booze they found back in the warehouses, the nuns saved the orphans, the cotton bales were torched and the wind blew, and the city burned.

9.

I was sixteen when my youth director bought me a copy of *Southern by the Grace of God*. I was twenty before I realized that it didn't belong on my bookshelf.

10.

The most monstrous barbarity of the barbarous march. Nobody talks about the lack of historic marker that tells the other part of it all. They don't mention the jubilation that came about with Sherman's arrival for most of the people who saw it.

11.

I'm talking about black people.

12.

Whenever they heard my name, they clustered about my horse, shouted and prayed. It's a tough thing: making sense of a story in hindsight, when no one could even really make any sense of it when it was happening. Smoke lingers. It saturates us. Gets in our pores and makes a mess of the memory of things. We like to say that Sherman had it out for us because of the early trouble we caused over at the Baptist Church, but that never really was the full truth of it all, and I think we knew that. We also knew he was careless with fire. But we'd heard tales of him gallivanting about around

Sullivan's Island and even talking friendly with a lady down in Savannah, or was it Augusta? I guess it doesn't really matter. The point is that we'd heard stories about him smiling all over the South before the war, and we never could really find a way to make sense of such a thing. The bright-eyed, red-headed man who'd burned down the South had to be a heartless son of a bitch. He needed to have scales.

12.

The red-headed stranger had eyes like thunder, and his lips, they were sad and tight. His little lost love lay asleep on the hillside, and his heart was heavy at night. Don't cross him. Don't boss him. He's wild in his sorrow. He's ridin' an' hidin his pain. Don't fight him. Don't spite him. Just wait till tomorrow. Maybe he'll ride on again.

13.

Southerners are not the only ones that mythologize the past. Sometimes that thought is refreshing. Sometimes I could care less.

14.

The younger versions of our grandparents knew better than to kill Yankees with the toy guns they bought in the checkout lines of the grocery store. Those guns were for Indian killing. That was the acceptable type of play for respectable young Southerners. The imaginary Yankees were saved for the older rednecks that still like to dress up in grey wool on the weekends. Back then, most of the kids seemed to barely care, or notice. They were too busy fighting on Wounded Knee every Saturday afternoon. It wasn't until Nintendo came out with their version of *The Civil War* that kids found out how much fun it was to let Johnny Reb win. *As God is my witness, they're not going to lick me.*

15.

I was up late watching the History channel and they had one of those bad BBC-style documentaries going. It was one of the ones where you can't tell if it's the actors that are moving in dramatic slow motion, or if it's the special effects that are making it look like that. The whole thing was on the last years of the war and the march. Sleep still hadn't found me when they made it to Columbia, and I watched as Confederate soldiers burned railroad stations. They then went on and burned Congaree River Bridge and a hell of a lot of cotton. And that's when this official sounding voice was piped in over the broadcast and told us all of this was done in accordance with Confederate policy. I got up the next morning, and drove down past the old train depot for a cup of coffee. The actors and their torches were gone.

16.

Everything you thought you knew can be changed with the right thought planted in you just so.

17.

War is a terrible thing... You are bound to fail. Only in your spirit and determination are you prepared for war. War is hell, and Sherman made war total. He brought the hell home. He took the spirit and determination that he saw in us, and set it on fire until we didn't have a choice but to come in and start setting a few more flames. When it was all said-and-done, that spirit had been burned down to the ground twice, and the only thing left was the smoke. And we sat in that smoke and built the story the way that our toddlers stack blocks. The pieces sat on each other like last night's dishes and rose out of that smoke without ever really figuring out their foundation or their eventual height.

18.

This is the tale of the red-headed stranger. The lines in this story have never been crisp. Sherman burned the South to the ground. He buried our homes and buildings in ashes the same way we buried Berlin and Hiroshima in theirs. He burned Columbia. And we've never seen a picture of him smiling. But that's not why we're really pissed at him. There are enough builders down here to get over that. We're pissed because we hid in our bathtubs and sat in the smoke, and we were too damned bitter to be happy for the people that were clustered about his horse, shouting and praying.

19.

Not every kid in the South chooses the grey soldiers when they play that Nintendo game.

EYE WITNESS COMES FORTH YEARS LATER

By Rachel Haynie

How long I had been obscured there, I still have no idea, but it was far too long a time to be face down in Mrs. Gibbes' garden dirt, rooting a row of boxwood hedges in place. Somehow the awkward way I was dropped there, at the perimeter of the property, left me just one nostril away from asphyxiation.

I can't tell you who finally found me or whether I was immediately returned to some member of the Gibbes family. Although the family home burned that dreadful February night, that corner - at Hampton and Plain (note: now Sumter) streets - continued to be called, for some time, "where Dr. Gibbes lived and had his medical practice." Whoever I was taken to, once I was found, surely must have been stunned to discover that I had survived.

Going back to the early twilight of a tumultuous night, I also have no idea whether it was friend or foe that jostled me out of Dr. Gibbes' library. If a family member caught me as my pedestal dissolved into ashes in the fire, got me outside and rolled me into the bushes for safekeeping, he or she must have forgotten where I was left because, even when the smoke cleared, days later, no one came back for me. I am no light-weight, so if it was a family member, it would have been one of Dr. Gibbes' sons. It would have been too much for one of the daughters to have lifted me and moved me stealthily out of harm's way.

Had it been one of Dr. Gibbes' few – but loyal, at least up to that point - slaves who escaped the flames with me in tow, seems he or she eventually would have let someone know where I was. Unless it was a she who had tired of dusting me weekly and figured with me out of the way, there'd be less objects to dust. I was surely the least of her worries; Dr. Gibbes had collections of so many things. Wonder how many dusting feathers were worn down by their quills, just taking care of those items?

It is possible that if I was saved by a he-servant, he bobbled me into the bushes and kept walking. I heard that when marauding Yankees told slaves they were free, a good many took their leave, never looking back. How hard would it have been to skulk away from a burning house, a fine one that for many years had been your home, and not even look back as the huge roof thundered, then imploded into the home's well-appointed interior.

Had it been a Blue-uniformed foe that wrested me from my pedestal, my place of prominence in a museum-like home unlike any other in the Southeast, the purpose of removing me may have been to wreak more havoc, in any way possible. Even drunk intruders would have realized the moment they attempted to lift me that I would not have been as easy to carry as smaller valuables, the sort of booty with which they had gouged their pockets at previous homes where they had stopped for spoils of war before they reached the culturally-rich Gibbes home.

It would have taken a most astute soldier, likely better educated – so perhaps an officer - to take me down and out solely to assure I could not continue in my role as eye witness to the mayhem being wrought that heartless night.

I saw it all. Every transgression that transpired in Dr. Gibbes' fine home on February 17 happened before my very fixed eyes. I witnessed villains ripping spectacular paintings out of frames with the tips of their swords. I saw them tumble hundreds of items from the good doctor's paleontology collection out of their cases and onto the floor, watched them stomp his conch collection with their boots, turning the shells into small mounds of sand. I watched his books and priceless papers curl into brown tendrils as flames licked the shelves on which they were carefully stored.

I am the bust of Dr. Robert Wilson Gibbes, and I am proud of it. My likeness, sculpted by Hiram Powers, is that of a brilliant physician, a scientist, an editor of fairly-told truth and contributor to many scholarly journals, a patron of the arts, and a multi-faceted collector. The man on whom I was based was so highly regarded by his peers he was referred to as The Mind of the South. Such superlatives would be hard for a bust to live up to. But I feel I have. And continue to from my current pedestal at Columbia Museum of Art.

From the time Powers blew the last marble dust off my face and delivered me to Gibbes, who immediately placed me on a pedestal of fine wood, I have kept vigil in his home. Long before South Carolina seceded from the Union, setting off a chain reaction, Gibbes had taken his leave from time to time, to attend professional conferences or meet with other scientists or other editors, and from time to time to return briefly to Charleston where he had grown up, and where he sustained valued friendships. Early in the '60s (that's the 1860s) his sense of duty called him away from home as well.

On that fateful day, Dr. Gibbes had left his home to attend emergencies related to his office as Surgeon General for South Carolina. Would he have left, even for duty, had he not believed the word Sherman gave Mayor Goodwyn when the city was peacefully surrendered? I think not! I heard Dr. Gibbes tell a neighbor Sherman had promised the mayor Columbia residences would exempt from the ruinous acts planned. For Gibbes, as for Goodwyn, a man's word was his bond. So, you can well imagine: when the first plunderers arrived on the scene, I wobbled on my pedestal.

Moments earlier, from out on the street Yankee soldiers lobbed rag-stuffed bottles of turpentine onto the roof. One of Dr. Gibbes' servants doused the first fire with buckets of water. As the good doctor returned home, barely in time to assert salvation for his home and collections, Yankees were inside the living room, within my clear view, and when Dr. Gibbes tried to avert them, one of the villains yelled at him, "Let the damn thing burn." He did all he could, but before long I saw the poor man take leave, his shoulders slumped in defeat.

I was helpless. Art dissolved as the oil in the paints worked as incendiaries, their frames rendered as kindling. Up in smoke went autographs of patriots, leaders, artists who had attracted Dr. Gibbes' friendship and patronage, whose work he had ceremoniously collected over years. Also lost that night were documents authenticating pivotal military actions taken during the Revolutionary War, a fight for a different kind of liberty, won from a sovereign nation both North and South agreed had been behaving tyrannically.

Some of the fossils in the vast collection – such as those of the long-extinct mosasaur - that already had withstood thousands of years of potentially-destroying natural conditions, might have endured the fire, although their carefully-prepared paper labels certainly would not have. What was not afire, plunderers swept up by the armfuls, not even knowing of their scientific value, bent only on destruction of any culture binding this society together. Samples from collections of all sorts were carted away in hopes something monetary could be gained from it one day.

The heat was too intense for man to bear – although it didn't affect me. I could have stayed the course, ah, but my pedestal would have given way on me. To this day I believe if not for the perilous danger attendant to staying, Dr. Gibbes would never have abandoned his home.

Days later I overheard, from my hideaway in the hedges, passersby saying they wished to forget the bedlam, even while knowing full well they never would forget it. My opinion may be ignored, but I happen to think that night should not be forgotten. There were too many lessons to be learned from it. My opinion came out of the quarry the same time I did. I am Cararra marble, you see, and my Italian origins share some proximity with the home of Cicero, although the chunk of marble from which I was sculpted was brought up from the mine thousands of years later (I did not assume my shapely form until centuries after Cicero pontificated.)

Around Cararra, as is true throughout Italy and I understand the entire world, Cicero's advice still holds sway. "Not to know what happened before you were born is to forever remain a child." So my advice is to follow Cicero's admonition and keep the history of that dreadful February night alive by retelling what happened, as accurately as possible, to any who will listen. There certainly was a lot of confusion that night, but there also were plenty of eye witnesses. You may count me among them.

Dr. Gibbes only lived another year and a half after he experienced those great losses. I had not been rescued at that point. Belatedly, my diagnosis? Cause of death: a broken heart more so than the pleurisy that had dogged him in years prior to the outbreak of the Civil War. He was laid to rest next to his wife in the graveyard at Trinity Episcopal Church. He has been active in his church, active in the community – twice he served as mayor – and long after he departed as a student, and even after his appointment on the faculty at South Carolina College, he remained active on boards and committees. Even before he distinguished himself in those civic and academic ways, he was highly regarded in medical circles and in the field of paleontology.

As for me, you ask? Ultimately, I was donated to the Columbia Museum of Art by one of Dr. Gibbes' descendants, who perpetuated the physician legacy and also bore his great-grandfather's first and last name, although his middle initial, W, stood for a sir name other than Wilson.

The pedestal on which I now stand sentinel is in Gallery 11. I hold up my corner in the American Gallery. Here among the decorative arts, the Scarborough portrait of Dr. Gibbes is my nearest neighbor. The Scarborough would not be with me here had that painting not been on loan to a family friend at the time of Sherman's Burning of Columbia.

If you come by to see me at Columbia Museum of Art and ask me if I still concur with what Cicero said, that we all will remain uninformed children forever if we do not learn of our past, you will not hear me disagree.

STARS

By Ed Madden

bullets in the dining room table and such

Never fixed, just six of them—
bronze stars affixed, bolted in,

a bronze for every occasion, cannon,

each mortar shell that picked a spot,
nicked the wall, its Winnsboro blue

(eleven shades of blue and grey)—

or knocked off a pediment, clipped
that window sill that's still watching west,

botched up the façade with a bang,
a burn, a fist of rust that burnished

the stone, pockmarked, permanent, done.

THE BURNING QUESTION

A SCREENPLAY

By James D. McCallister

EXTERIOR CAMPUS — The tree-shaded Horseshoe at the University of South Carolina. A venerable old classroom building. Comings and goings, backpacks, staring at smart-phones, etc.

HISTORIAN "... and with their usage as makeshift hospitals, many buildings that you know from the old campus called 'The Horseshoe,' survived the occupation and burning of the city the night of February 17, 1865."

INTERIOR CLASSROOM — Half full of budding Southern historians listening to the Historian's lecture. As he speaks, we also get a look at one particular student (FILMMAKER) sitting in the far back row, perhaps a little older than the rest of the class. He does not have a notebook.

HISTORIAN "Otherwise, the city of Columbia lost most all its vital downtown commercial district. Homes, businesses, municipal buildings, railroads, bridges. Walking around our lovely small city on a nice, sunny afternoon, we can scarcely imagine such devastation... but with warfare as an ongoing concern of humanity the world over, there are places today that certainly can."

STUDENT (raising hand) "So the Union troops came through and just torched the place even though there wasn't a battle per se? Harsh, dude."

HISTORIAN "Maybe they did, and maybe they didn't. It's likely, sure. Bear in mind, though, that thanks to the passage of time, the fog of war, and political interpretations of events surrounding the 17th of February, agreement among historians on whose version of events should stand has been difficult to reconcile."

STUDENT "Isn't that true of any ancient history? That we can't witness ourselves?"

HISTORIAN "Yes. If we can call something that happened only 150 years ago 'ancient.' And I'm not sure we should."

STUDENT "Yo, five minutes ago is ancient to me."

The class, very young, laughs in knowing agreement. More than half of them react without looking up from the screens of the various devices on their desks. The HISTORIAN is nodding and patient with her young charges.

HISTORIAN "As to the specifics of your question, in the case of the burning of Columbia we have primary eyewitness accounts and memoirs and even congressional testimony by participants, given under oath, to go on. If we believe certain points of view, like that of the writer William Gilmore Simms, there's no question that Union troops arrived here with at least tacit orders to make the city feel their presence and power. Others blame the widespread fire on fleeing Confederate troops who lit aflame cotton and other stores to keep the Yankees from getting the materiel for themselves. Still others talk of Union troops helping to fight the fires; while others are described as drunken, lascivious, and destructive."

STUDENT "What do you mean 'tacit?'"

HISTORIAN "Let's see. As in, someone in authority not saying yes, but not saying no, either. Turning a blind eye. Get it?"

Murmuring and nodding. The Historian glances at the time, then makes eye contact with the FILMMAKER.

HISTORIAN "But as we're up against it today, we'll get into the specifics next time, as well as getting Sherman out of South Carolina and on toward the end of the war. Papers due end of next week. Don't wait till the last minute... (a knowing smile) like I always did. Laughter and bustling as the class breaks up."

EXTERIOR CAMPUS — The FILMMAKER AND HISTORIAN do a walk and talk through the picturesque, well-preserved campus. Their body language is comfortable — they know each other. Perhaps there's budding attraction underneath all the scholarly banter.

HISTORIAN "So how's the film script coming along?"

FILMMAKER "Not bad. Appreciate you letting me listen in today. Trying to sort through my ideas."

HISTORIAN "So tell me."

FILMMAKER "I had the notion to try to make the whole burning of the city exciting, somehow."

HISTORIAN (snorting) "You mean more 'exciting' than it probably was?"

FILMMAKER (frustrated) "Ya know. Give us a sense of human drama and conflict. Not like these modern movies where cities are getting destroyed for the spectacle of it all.

They cross the street, enter the State House grounds.

HISTORIAN "All right. Specifics, and conflict. You heard it in our classroom discussion earlier regarding the truth of how the city burned. On one hand, an army — an enemy army — rolls up to the riverside, is met by the mayor, under direction of General Wade Hampton, to literally wave a white flag."

They pause near the African-American history monument.

FILMMAKER "If the Mayor surrendered the city in such a formal way, surely he thought this would prevent the wholesale destruction that followed."

HISTORIAN "Supposedly all would be orderly, and barring resistance from retreating Confederate forces, which by then were few in number, no one need worry about undue violence or plundering. At least that was the gist of a letter dispatched from Mayor Goodwyn to General Sherman asking that a sufficient guard be sent in advance of the rest of the army to ensure the protection of civilians and private property. Of course, looting by both Confederate soldiers and poor citizens, both white and freed black slaves, had already been going on."

FILMMAKER "Sounds like the city was in big trouble even before Sherman arrived."

HISTORIAN "It was chaos. War is not pretty."

FILMMAKER "I wish there were some unspoiled locations. Charleston, you can really do some recreations on actual locations. Here... not so much."

HISTORIAN "True; but as Walter Edgar says, in the years since 1865 Columbians themselves have razed more ante-bellum architecture than was burned that night, and in the name of 'progress.'"

FILMMAKER "Still, it's so hard to imagine the city back then. Like, impossible. Look at this place now."

Montage of busy city streets. Activity. Modernity.

HISTORIAN "For a location that hasn't changed much, we can take a look at the Congaree Creek area, where the last battles were fought prior to the Union troops taking Columbia."

FILMMAKER "Actual Civil War battles, now we're talking. I think that's where I was getting hung up — how to dramatize the conflict of a victorious army rolling in essentially unopposed... and still ending up trashing the place."

HISTORIAN "What you had at Congaree Creek were skirmishes with greatly diminished, though tenacious and honorable Confederate troops. A failing army fighting for a losing cause, holding out in vain. And uncertain if Sherman were even coming, until only days before. Distances were greater back then. Information didn't flow so instantaneously. Ten miles away was much farther than we think of it now."

FILMMAKER "What do you say to taking a stroll out there?"

HISTORIAN "Today?"

FILMMAKER "Why not?"

HISTORIAN "I could be bribed with a coffee."

FILMMAKER "Can-do."

They pass by the Confederate Memorial Monument on their way to Main Street. Pull back to REVEAL the battle flag hanging high in its place of prominence.

EXTERIOR DIRT ROAD AND CONGAREE CREEK — MONTAGE
We see the soldier in question that the Filmmaker describes engaging in some of this activity: bandaged and bloody, waking up in the bushes, stumbling along a dirt road, etc.

FILMMAKER (Voice Over) "My big idea was to have a soldier, a Union infantryman, who's late to the party, so to speak.

He's behind the rest of Sherman's regiment, the XVth Corps, trying to catch up. He's — he's been hurt. Maybe it's in this battle you were talking about, out at the creek. He's grazed, crawls off into the bushes and his dudes leave him behind by accident. He comes to — has to catch up — or maybe: he doesn't want to catch up. He's had enough. The burning that he knows is coming is too much for him. What they're planning to do."

HISTORIAN (Voice Over) "A humanistic soldier instead of a vengeful one bent on mayhem?"

EXTERIOR COFFEE SHOP — The two having their coffees. The City is ALIVE all around them.

FILMMAKER "Right. A conscientious objector. So to speak."

HISTORIAN "Now there's some conflict for you. Desertion, a serious military crime."

FILMMAKER "What if he has a loved one in the city, and is worried about her safety? A Southern girlfriend."

HISTORIAN "A historical romance? I wouldn't know the first thing about all that." Eye contact. "Maybe another layer to all this, peeking through."

FILMMAKER "A great romance does a story good. That's what they say."

EXTERIOR VARIOUS — DRIVING MONTAGE Getting them out to the park. Evocative images contrasting the modern with the natural world. It's a contrast of modern conveniences compared to the descriptions of the deprivations of life as a soldier: FILMMAKER (Voice Over) "From what I've read, these troops were pissed off because of having to slog through the swamps of the lowcountry to get here. Nasty weather."

HISTORIAN (Voice Over) "That's true. It had been a cold and wet February. Sherman's men were battle– and weather-hardened by this point. It's easy to speculate that they felt as though their long march through Georgia were about to culminate here in South Carolina. The taking of Columbia could be seen as one of the death-blows to the Confederacy."

EXTERIOR PARKING LOT (OLD STATE ROAD) — Atmospheric. The day is waning, the light changing. End state maintenance sign. Old growth trees. Bird calls. Spooky. A walk and talk on the old dirt road.

FILMMAKER "What exactly happened out here?"

HISTORIAN "The Rebels had constructed what the Federals found to be impressive fortifications ten to fifteen feet in height, and a twenty-five foot moat along the creek. Shelling, firefights. The greatest clusters of spent casings found by archeologists indicate where the ferocity of the fighting was at its height. A foggy day."

FILMMAKER "So they're defending the southern approach to the city, the capital city of the state. The heart of the Confederacy, in its way."

HISTORIAN "The 'seat of Secession,' as Columbia had been called."

FILMMAKER "But that word — 'ferocity'. It must've been a battle and a half."

HISTORIAN "Not by the numbers. Near as we can tell, thirty-three Confederates and half a dozen Union soldiers died, with other casualties. By the standards of the war? Low intensity. Except to the dead..."

FILMMAKER "And the wounded. I don't want the film to be Civil War wound-porn, though."

HISTORIAN "Maybe that's your movie? It's not about the burning of Columbia, rather, what it felt like to be on the outskirts of the conflagration...?"

FILMMAKER "It's symbolic: in the way that we can't see what really happened from our vantage point here in the future, we'll view the events of that day and night through the point of view of this soldier who's not in the thick of things. Who doesn't quite witness it all."

HISTORIAN (unsure about this) "Symbolic, huh? Like what they now call a psy-op?"

FILMMAKER "Shock and awe type stuff."

HISTORIAN "The confederacy's nominal seat, burned and trampled and trammeled into submission. 'The truth is the whole army is burning with an insatiable desire to wreak vengeance upon South Carolina," as Sherman wrote to

Major General Halleck in December 1864. Few believed it in Columbia, not even among the Confederate generals, but in a way everyone should've seen Columbia's destruction as inevitable."

FILMMAKER "What happened after the battle of Congaree Creek?"

HISTORIAN "The remaining Southern troops retreated toward the city, which was lightly defended by Wheeler's Cavalry, who also unfortunately participated in the looting of the wealthy city's shops. They burned bridges and made the going as slow as possible for the Federals. But essentially, by the 17th of February, the city is completely undefended."

FILMMAKER (snaps fingers) "Oh, that's it. My soldier, who's left behind, can't catch up with his battalion because the bridges are burned."

HISTORIAN "Burning the bridges slowed down Sherman's experienced Union soldiers, as did an overnight bombardment of their encampment that supposedly angered Sherman. They reach a modern bridge over the Congaree Creek. The real symbolic moment for me, though, has to do with the massing of the Federals on the Western side of the Congaree. It was said to be an imposing spectacle of marching troops, bands playing, flags snapping in the breeze. All in full view of the city on the other side."

FILMMAKER "Must've been terrifying for the residents and refugees. I'm not sure we have the budget to dramatize all that anyway. Doesn't seem like enough for someone to just hear about it, though. Something like that should be seen."

HISTORIAN "You could do it with CGI, like they do those superhero movies with the cities crumbling."

FILMMAKER "Hah. Maybe someday. Must be nice to have the tools and the talent and the money to realize images like that."

HISTORIAN (musing philosophical) "Words, language, paintings, films — these are abstractions we use to translate and describe our experience of the real world. In our case, the observable world. To the historian, she spends much of her time describing the nonobservable past that existed, once, like the circumstances of the battle on this very ground. Not so easy to do. We must rely on the historical record. People's interpretations and memories. And our imaginations, to a large extent. I suppose the idea of a historian with a good imagination could be seen as undesirable..."

FILMMAKER "Nothing undesirable about it." Contemplating the blackwater creek. Birdcalls and the chirr of cicadas in the trees. A peaceful moment. "So: Our man, in the woods, lost... he just wants to beat these Confederates. Get home. Maybe he would have been mad. Mad enough to burn the town down."

HISTORIAN "Only the dead could tell us how they felt. What they experienced. What they said. Sherman. Simms. Wade Hampton. Emma LeConte. The soldiers. 'Your man,' as you keep calling him."

FILMMAKER "My man's not a bad guy. He wouldn't set the city on fire just to get home. But a good soldier, he'd do what his orders were."

HISTORIAN "Warfare has a way of altering how we think of right and wrong. And symbolic behavior is often rooted in mob-rule mentality."

FILMMAKER "C'mon. We're losing the light. It's probably haunted out here at night."

HISTORIAN "That's what they say." She reacts to something off-screen. "Or maybe during the day, too. Friend of yours?"

FILMMAKER (squinting) "Huh?"

EXTERIOR PARKING LOT — As they approach, a figure standing near the car: A soldier! In blue! With a head wound!

HISTORIAN "Maybe he could answer a few of our questions."

FILMMAKER "Holy crap — is that — him?"

HISTORIAN “Looks like our man. Told you I have a good imagination. (To the Soldier) Evening, sir. We come not as the enemy — we’re civilians.”

SOLDIER “Aye, that I see.”

FILMMAKER “Maybe we could ask you a few questions...?”

SOLDIER “Dead men tell no tales.”

HISTORIAN “How about the truth, then?”

SOLDIER “Do the best I can, ma’am.”

FILMMAKER “This is a lucky break. Except that, if this is ‘my man,’ then he doesn’t know anything about the burning of the city — for him, it hasn’t happened yet.”

SOLDIER “Aye, did they go and burn that hole of Secession after all?”

HISTORIAN “Ah-ha. Now we’re getting somewhere.” The moment holds. The soldier is unsteady on his feet. Injured. The Filmmaker looks at his hands, clean and neat and smooth. At the Soldier’s hands: scabbed and bloody.

FILMMAKER “Were you guys ordered to burn Columbia?”

SOLDIER “Only the public buildings and manufacturing works of the enemy, sir.”

HISTORIAN “What’s it been like to be a soldier fighting under this General? How do you feel about the war?”

SOLDIER (matter of fact) "It's hell, ma'am. Pure-T hell being in war. You ever had anyone shooting at you before?" The Soldier winces, touches his bandaged head.

HISTORIAN "You feel like telling us about it?"

SOLDIER "Not especially. But if you want."

FILMMAKER "We'll give you a ride the rest of the way into town."

HISTORIAN "Tell us about Congaree Creek..." The vehicle, driving away down Old State Road, back toward the city, a brilliant orange-red sunset... In both the east and western skies.

SOLDIER "The rebs had a good solid fort built up there, but didn't put up much of a fight, not really. What ones did was no slouches. Just not enough of 'em. They put they best into the fight like anyone would. But like most of us, they's just boys, drafted up and without no dog in the fight outside of the battlefield. And I doubt that many on either side by that point wanted much in fighting no more."

HISTORIAN "You fellas were told to really give Columbia that 'hell' you talked about? Because of who she was to the confederacy?"

SOLDIER "What d'ya mean?"

INTERIOR CAR — SOLDIER in the passenger seat, FILMMAKER driving, HISTORIAN leaning forward from the rear seat —

HISTORIAN "Because the war began here. When South Carolina, the first to secede—"

SOLDIER "Oh, aye. Yeah, we all knew this was where it began. And maybe where it was all down to. Maybe not in a military sense. The Rebels, they was well-nigh on retreated from here."

FILMMAKER "We would call it 'symbolic', the destruction of the city."

HISTORIAN "Not to mention the eastern idea of karma. That wrongs perpetuated are eventually balanced out by—"

SOLDIER "Aye, aye. We got a saying. What goes around—"

HISTORIAN "—comes around?"

The Soldier, smiling and nodding, maybe an anachronistic THUMB'S UP.

FILMMAKER "Yeah, we have that one too."

SOLDIER "If all this mess started here, you can imagine how emotions was running. Knowing that we had managed to roll all the way up to this here river of yourn. We felt powerful."

FILMMAKER "Revenge might've been in the air."

SOLDIER "There might've been talk like that. You so and sos, we're a-gonna give you what-for. Like I told you, though. Most of us at this point just want to get home in one piece. Columbia's on the way, or at least General Sherman's taking us that way. So no matter what any one of us might've figured on doing along the way, what we wrought was gonna come."

FILMMAKER "But did it have to happen? Like it did? My buddy back here tells me that most of the opposing forces had retreated and left Columbia to surrender. Nothing but wounded troops and old people and kids left behind. That was raw, bro."

SOLDIER "Don't blame me." He gestures to the eastern sky glowing amber. "I'm late to the hoe-down. You wouldn't want to be blamed for something you hadn't done. Would you?"

FILMMAKER "No."

HISTORIAN "Definitely not."

SOLDIER "Not a one of us is there to see what's happening. Not you, not me. None of us three."

HISTORIAN "All we can do is sift the ashes and imagine. Whether it's correspondence from various figures, Sherman's testimony under oath, Simms's aggrieved narrative, or Emma LeConte's diary, only those who lived through the burning of Columbia can remotely know how it occurred, what it felt like. And these narratives, they were often those of the elite classes. The war's dreadful effects on other classes of people who may lack a voice in the historical record, in particular the slaves themselves, remains less imaginable without their voices to tell the story."

FILMMAKER "Like we don't have a clue what it feels like to have served and fought in war."

SOLDIER "Lookit: Don't spend too much time imagining that stuff. Not if you don't have to. War is nothing to be imagining."

EXTERIOR ROADWAY INTO COLUMBIA — Magic hour. The glow from the east isn't from a fire, it's the spectacular reflection from the skyline of the setting sun to the west.

SOLDIER "The times of war and burning and conflict, them's the bad times. Do you have enough to eat? Do you have your loved ones nearby? Are people free...?"

FILMMAKER "For the most part. Things aren't so bad here in Columbia now. In fact..."

HISTORIAN " ...they're very well. Quite well indeed."

A HOMELESS PERSON is seen on a side street. The trio inside the car again.

HISTORIAN "But could always be better."

SOLDIER "That's what you got to remember. No matter how bad it gets, no matter how much you hurt... there's always a better tomorrow. Just like how this place rebuilt itself. Looks really nice, too."

EXTERIOR CAMPUS. The vehicle, pulling into a street space.

FILMMAKER "Well, we're really lucky to have found someone with such an enlightened..."

INTERIOR CAR. But surprise - The SOLIDER has now disappeared.

FILMMAKER "...and philosophically inclined worldview."

HISTORIAN "Funny how convenient that was. It's almost as though our words conjured him up."

FILMMAKER "Our imaginative abstractions? Like in some movie?" A warm smile between these colleagues, modern citizens of Columbia, SC, indeed, a long way from the time of war and suffering.

HISTORIAN "Here's my big question: is there really a movie? Or do you just like hanging out with me."

FILMMAKER "Put it like this: I still don't have my story, not really. But I'm closer. Maybe the real burning question is this: want to go grab a bite?"

HISTORIAN "Haven't had enough of me yet?"

FILMMAKER "Not by any stretch of the imagination."

More warmth.

FADE OUT.

AT 16, THOMAS MAY AS WELL CONSIDER BOTANY

By Ray McManus

No one sees the weed, its long arm raised to ask the sky its question, and even the sky looks the other way. Something familiar, perhaps as a sprout at first, the way roots take their hold just long enough to push back – my father, his father before – scattered. The rest is just work. The rest is just a story about dry rot, brown skin windswept coarse and etched by line and plaster. Should I measure my height by the way wood stains, or what works its way through grain, through gaps in boards swollen with the weight of rain like a stick pointed at the eye of God? Somewhere in this story, a prayer soaked in humid bravado with no place to go, a note on what it takes to stand there without permission, its silhouette cast on the wall from the city burning behind it. This much I know. This is a shadow. And no one sees me.

DAYS UNTIL REVENGE? 1,522
COLUMBIA WAS A TARGET FROM THE START

By Tom Poland

When secessionists dreamed of a confederacy, a new country, had it been written "The Impossible Dream" would have served as a song of admonition, for its lyrics capture the daunting task facing the South. *To dream the impossible dream, to fight the unbeatable foe, to bear with unbearable sorrow...*

No song would divert the South from its cause and the dream-turned-nightmare destroyed a beautiful city, one that would never recapture its early garden-rich glory. It was inevitable that Columbia would get the torch. Pink Floyd's "Dogs of War" laid out what was coming ... *The dogs of war don't negotiate, the dogs of war won't capitulate, they will take and you will give....*

William Tecumseh Sherman said that he didn't order Columbia's burning but surely he knew his men intended to burn the city. As soon as they crossed the Savannah River, they began to torch South Carolina. From history's archives, telling reports, quotes, and passages indicate Columbia was a target for destruction from the start.

Blazing Numbers

12-17-1860

Columbia's First Baptist Church hosts the South Carolina Secession Convention.

2-17-1865

General Sherman's forces roll into Columbia.

2-18-1865

A firestorm sweeps through Columbia.

1,522

The number of days that passed from the Secession Convention to the burning of the city.

On December 24, 1864, Sherman wrote to Major General Halleck in Washington saying that he was now "free to make a broad swath through South and North Carolina. The truth is, the whole army is burning with an insatiable desire to wreak vengeance upon South Carolina. I almost tremble at her fate, but feel that she deserves all that seems in store for her."

"With Savannah in our possession, at some future time, if not now, we can punish South Carolina as she deserves ... I do sincerely believe that the whole United States, north and south, would rejoice to have this army turned loose on South Carolina, to devastate that State ... it would have a direct and immediate bearing on your campaign in Virginia." —Report to General Grant from General Sherman.

"There was a grim determination on the part of the men in the ranks to visit a severe judgment on South Carolina ... We practically burned a swath 60 miles wide across ...The Commanders were powerless ... This destruction of property was a matter of revenge." —Private John C. Arbuckle, Company K, Fourth Iowa Veteran Volunteer Infantry

"In all of our campaigns, no other city in the South awakened our interest and bad feeling as did this city of Columbia; and now, here it was, with all of its beauty and attractiveness, in full view; but, withal, this was the trouble, there attached to it the bad eminence of having been the first of Southern Capitols to lead off in unleashing the dogs of war ... The sacrifice, blood and carnage of four years of war through which we had passed, were due to what first took place here in the city of Columbia. Judging from the temper and feeling of the men in the ranks, it was evident that a terrible day of retribution had at last come to this beleaguered and doomed city." —Private John C. Arbuckle

"The well-known sight of columns of black smoke meets our gaze again; this time houses are burning, and South Carolina has commenced to pay an installment ... on her debt to justice and humanity. With the help of God, we will have principal and interest before we leave her borders ... Where our footsteps pass, fire, ashes, and desolation follow in the path." —Major George Ward Nichols, Sherman's aide-de-camp

"Universal license to burn and plunder was the order of the day." —Union Officer Thomas G. Myers

"I have never doubted that Columbia was deliberately set on fire in more than a hundred places." —Union General William B. Hazen

"If I had made up my mind to burn Columbia I would have burnt it with no more feeling than I would a common prairie dog village; but I did not do it ..." —General William Tecumseh Sherman

In fairness to Sherman, the historian Alan Nevins described the change that came over Sherman's army when it crossed the Savannah and sensed it was heading northward toward home. "Every soldier felt he was in the heart of the enemy's country and it was his duty to do all the damage possible to the enemy." Nevins quoted a veteran of the march. "Houses were set on fire so near the road ... it became so hot our ammunition trains were obliged to go out in the fields to pass. If we halted to rest in a little town, it would be but a short time before houses all about seemed to be in flames." The scene was repeated "all across the state.'" Not only did no one have orders to do this work of destruction, but on the contrary it was strictly forbidden.'" Yet it happened. An Illinois major recalled, "The army burnt everything that it came near in South Carolina, not under orders but in spite of orders."

Final Word

In "New Views on the Burning of Columbia," James Reston Jr. wrote of Sherman: "His mission was terror. Call it genius or knavery, but it was Sherman's loose control over his army as it passed through Columbia that produced the element of terror he sought. His alternating states of talkativeness and taciturnity the night of the fire may have indicated a man who had lost control, but that very lapse led to a desired effect. Likewise the kid-glove treatment accorded Savannah, after the burning of Atlanta and before the call on Columbia, may have induced a state of hopefulness in some, but its real offspring was the kind of terror that comes from not knowing, a state of mind that makes planning impossible and puts incredible strain on leadership.

"Sherman's mission, as it was carried out in Columbia, profoundly affected the psychology of the North, too. By burning Columbia or letting it burn, Sherman gave his countrymen what they had been craving for nearly four years of war--clear and unadulterated victory, compounded of the defeat and punishment of the enemy."

TECUMSEH

By Tom Poland

Who Was This Man Who Claimed To Love South Carolina?

When I think of the burning of Columbia, I see William Tecumseh Sherman astride his horse on a hill near 12th Street, a great vantage point. Steadying his horse, he trains his spyglass beyond the Congaree on "the capital of the haughty state that instigated and forced forward the treason, which has brought on this desolating war." That's how Tecumseh's aide-de-camp, Major George Ward Nichols, put it. Tecumseh had no quarrel with that sentiment for he and his men viewed South Carolina as "the cause of their woes," thoroughly deserving destruction and destroy it they did.

Who was Tecumseh, the Union general whose visit made Columbia famously hot in February 1865?

His family called him Cump and his dad ironically bestowed Tecumseh upon him due to a fascination with the Shawnee leader of a tribal confederacy that opposed the United States. His troops called him Uncle Billy with affection.

Born February 8, 1820, in Lancaster, Ohio, Tecumseh fell under the zodiac sign Aquarius. Aquarians are noted for being humanitarians. So much for astrology. This Aquarian engineered a Scorched Earth strategy that cut the

Confederacy in half and inflicted $1.4 billion in modern economy destruction on Georgia and South Carolina. To this day his name evokes rancor.

Tecumseh was 45 years old when he led Union troops into Columbia. His penmanship was beautiful. As for him? Well, if you see photographs of Tecumseh, you'll judge him a bit scruffy with his punkish tousled red hair. He reminds me of Gordon Sumner of Police fame.

Tecumseh came from good stock and he was bright. His father sat on the Ohio Supreme Court, and Tecumseh graduated from West Point sixth of forty-two. In 1840, he entered the Army as a second lieutenant in the 3rd U.S. Artillery. As fate would have it, he began his military career down South. He fought in the Second Seminole War in the big gator peninsula and spent time in Georgia and South Carolina where he was assigned in 1842 to garrison duty at Fort Moultrie.

Outgoing, polished, and the foster son of Thomas Ewing, a prominent Whig politician from Ohio, this Sting-look-alike rubbed elbows with Charleston's upper circles. Tecumseh hunted, fished, boated, danced, and socialized with friends in Charleston and Sullivan's Island numerous times. He found South Carolina "so bright and delightful, that I have almost renounced all allegiance to Ohio, although it contains all whom I love and regard as friends."

Another Southern connection. His military career interrupted, in 1859, Tecumseh became the first superintendent of the Louisiana State Seminary of Learning & Military Academy. He did a good job and was well liked. (Later the institution became LSU. Imagine Tecumseh dressed up like a Crown Royal bag, all purple and gold, striding into Williams-Brice Stadium shouting "Geaux Tigers!") All his fun down South would soon end though. Events boiling up in Columbia and Charleston would see to that.

An Ominous Date

The 17th of the month hasn't been the best day for South Carolina's capital city. Columbia's First Baptist Church hosted the South Carolina Secession Convention December 17, 1860. A smattering of smallpox broke out and the convention adjourned to Charleston. There, three days later, South Carolina voted unanimously to leave the union, the first state to do so. A party-like atmosphere broke out in Columbia. The party would lead to utter disaster. If you want to tally the days until the Union would wreak vengeance on Columbia the number is 1,522. Come February 17, 1865, Tecumseh would invade Columbia. By the time he'd leave, 84 of the city's 124 blocks would have burned to the ground.

Secessionists' dream of a new country would become a nightmare, unleashing the deadliest war in the country's history and making Columbia a target from the start. The Confederate States of America would lose 258,000 men, the Union 360,222. In all, 618,222 men would die, and the deaths would continue after the war. Though General Robert E. Lee would surrender to General Ulysses S. Grant on

April 9, 1865, news of the surrender would take a while to get out. Among the last to die would be a soul who'd give up the ghost just 40 miles from Columbia. On April 18, 1865, at Boykin Mill near Stateburg fifteen-year-old Burwell Boykin would First Lieutenant E. L. Stevens of the 54th Massachusetts Infantry to death.

As for Tecumseh, he didn't object to slavery. In fact, he was sympathetic to Southerners' defense of slavery. He did not take lightly, however, to dissolving the Union, and he was a prophet of doom. When he heard South Carolina had seceded from the United States, he remarked to his friend and ardent secessionist, Professor David F. Boyd of Virginia: "You people of the South don't know what you are doing. This country will be drenched in blood, and God only knows how it will end. It is all folly, madness, a crime against civilization! You people speak so lightly of war; you don't know what you're talking about. War is a terrible thing! You mistake, too, the people of the North. They are a peaceable people but an earnest people, and they will fight, too. They are not going to let this country be destroyed without a mighty effort to save it ... Besides, where are your men and appliances of war to contend against them? The North can make a steam engine, locomotive, or railway car; hardly a yard of cloth or pair of shoes can you make. You are rushing into war with one of the most powerful, ingeniously mechanical, and determined people on Earth—right at your doors. You are bound to fail. Only in your spirit and determination are you prepared for war. In all else you are totally unprepared, with a bad cause to start with. At first you will make headway, but as your limited resources begin to fail, shut out from the markets of Europe as you will be, your cause will begin to wane. If your people will but stop and think, they must see in the end that you will surely fail."

When Louisiana became the sixth state to leave the Union January 26, 1861, Tecumseh resigned from what would become LSU and moved to St. Louis. He had no desire to participate in the war ... yet.

Three Months Later

April 12, 1861—Down Charleston way, Confederate General P. G. T. Beauregard ordered Fort Sumter's shelling. At 4:30 a.m. in predawn darkness, cannon fire reverberated throughout the city. Residents and the curious climbed to the rooftops of Battery homes to watch the action. The Civil War had arrived and it didn't take long to visit its ills on Tecumseh, who, after the firing on Fort Sumter, asked his brother, Senator John Sherman, to arrange a commission in the Army.

In May 1861, appointed colonel in the 13th U.S. Infantry, Tecumseh was assigned command of a brigade under General William McDowell in Washington, D.C. It was his fate to fight in the First Battle of Bull Run where Confederates routed Union troops. This thrashing at the hands of the Rebels must have shaken Tecumseh who was then sent to Kentucky where he became unrealistically pessimistic about the war. He griped to his superiors about shortages while overstating the enemy's strength. Placed on leave at his own request, he was considered unfit for duty. The press described him as "insane." It's believed Tecumseh suffered a nervous breakdown.

He persevered and returned to duty. Shiloh gave him his first test as a combat commander. Mindful of his Kentucky woes, rather than appear easily alarmed Tecumseh dismissed intelligence reports that Confederate General Albert Sidney Johnston was close by. He didn't shore up picket lines nor did he send out reconnaissance patrols. (I didn't want them think I was crazy.") On the morning of April 6, 1862, the Confederates brought hell itself to Union troops, but Tecumseh and Grant rallied their troops and repelled the Southern boys by day's end. Tecumseh was wounded twice—in the hand and shoulder—and had three horses shot out from under him. Reinforcements arrived overnight, and Union troops counterattacked the next morning, dispersing the Rebs. Shiloh bonded Tecumseh and Grant for life.

The war carried on. In March 1864 Tecumseh succeeded Grant as the commander in the west. In May, Tecumseh and 100,000 men advanced on Atlanta to engage Joseph E. Johnston's 60,000-strong Army of Tennessee. September 2, 1864. Tecumseh captured and burned Atlanta. He began his "March to the Sea," gloating, "I can make Georgia howl" and howl it did.

On December 21, 1864, Tecumseh arrived in Savannah leaving a 300-mile-long wake of destruction 60 miles wide. Tecumseh telegraphed Lincoln, offering him Savannah as a Christmas present.

Tecumseh then persuaded Grant to let him march north through the Carolinas, destroying everything of military value in his path, as he had done in Georgia. He particularly wanted to target South Carolina, that state "so bright and delightful, that I have almost renounced all allegiance to Ohio," because of the effect it would have on Southern morale. His army proceeded north getting light resistance from General Joseph E. Johnston's troops. Upon hearing that Tecumseh's men were advancing a dozen miles a day on corduroy roads through Salkehatchie swamps, Johnston "made up his mind that there had been no such army in existence since the days of Julius Caesar." That army would lay Columbia low and much of it would burn. Never mind that a neutral commission found that neither Federal nor Confederate officers intentionally or unintentionally burned the city. I say Tecumseh turned a blind eye to the burning of Columbia.

Tecumseh's scorched earth policy had begun in Mississippi. There Tecumseh and Grant's men burned the city of Jackson over and over until it earned the nickname "Chimneyville," for only chimneys remained. And yeah there was a lot of soot, just like in Columbia where the burning remains a mystery and controversy to this day.

In *South Carolina, A History*, Walter Edgar wrote, "It was accepted as gospel that Sherman laid waste to Columbia and twenty-one other towns, but in reality his forces left a considerable number of antebellum buildings unharmed. For example, about two-thirds of the capital city's pre-Civil War structures remained after the state's first experiment with urban renewal."

Sherman, who claimed evacuating Confederates started the raging fires, later wrote: "Though I never ordered it and never wished it, I have never shed any tears over the event, because I believe that it hastened what we all fought for, the end of the War."

Did a passive-aggressive Tecumseh permit Columbia to burn? Yes or no. Consider Tecumseh's quotes and arrive at your own decision.

This war differs from other wars, in this particular. We are not fighting armies but a hostile people, and must make old and young, rich and poor, feel the hard hand of war.

I would make this war as severe as possible, and show no symptoms of tiring till the South begs for mercy.

My aim, then, was to whip the rebels, to humble their pride, to follow them to their inmost recesses, and make them fear and dread us. Fear is the beginning of wisdom.

The truth is, the whole army is burning with an insatiable desire to wreak vengeance upon South Carolina. I almost tremble at her fate, but feel that she deserves all that seems in store for her.

Tecumseh's Death

Tecumseh died of pneumonia in New York City in the afternoon Saturday, 14 February 1891, six days shy of his 71st birthday. President Benjamin Harrison ordered all national flags to be flown at half-mast.

War makes for strange bedfellows. General Joseph E. Johnston, who fought Tecumseh's troops in Georgia and the Carolinas, served as a pallbearer for the old warrior. It was bitterly cold and a friend admonished Johnston to put on his hat, fearing the general might become ill. Johnston's reply? "If I were in [Sherman's] place, and he were standing in mine, he would not put on his hat."

Johnston died a month later of pneumonia.

Tecumseh sleeps for eternity in Calvary Cemetery in St. Louis. His memorials include the gilded bronze equestrian statue by Augustus Saint-Gaudens at the main entrance to Central Park and Carl Rohl-Smith's monument near President's Park in D.C. Other tributes include the World War II M4 Sherman tank and the "General Sherman" Giant Sequoia tree, the world's most massive documented single-trunk tree. Does he deserve these memorials? Maybe, maybe not.

I can't explain it but in writing this narrative I lost a bit of my distaste for Tecumseh despite the fact that I am a Georgian. He came across as a man who wasn't quite sure of his identity. He loved South Carolina as a twenty-two year old but we all know how much we change by our forties. He should have been more assured for he practiced "hard war" and many regard him as the first modern general.

I won't speak for South Carolina, but I will say this. Whatever he was or wasn't, to this day Tecumseh remains the most despised man in Georgia. "Vindictive and cruel," that's how Georgians describe Tecumseh. I'd add that he was bold. He married his foster sister, Ellen, a daring act that takes guts no matter the era.

UNTITLED

By Tara Powell

We rake the leaves back, carefully stack
Stones, spread gravel, make a tee-pee
Of sticks, and wait for it to catch.
Our son's green eyes darken with pleasure.
The sparks reflecting in them
Are constellations on rippling water.
The the the fire, he stutters, *is orange, is is is*
Dancing! He wrests his small body from
My arms and ricochets east to west and back
Again to each post of the fence hemming
Our backyard, trampling the long shades
Of autumn that thread the wisps of smoke
Haloing this year's little freedom fire.
Falo falo falo, we say in Italian. We practice
Counting twigs as I let him feed the flame,
And I try explaining about February 17,
And the long-awaited liberty his great-great-greats
Celebrated that night with bonfires that crowned
A mountain ghetto hemmed by stone beyond
The ragged ocean. He will need to know why
Our family is lighting a miniature *falo* alone
In our twilight corner of urban South
Carolina, why singing French psalms,
Why I am telling tales of ancient Italian politics

The same night Columbia remembers
Its own trial by fire, torched to terror
By drunkenness and greed, a city of sick men
And angry women thronged unbelievably
Behind the gates of the mental hospital,
Blistered with desire and some with fearful
Joy as well, clutching stunned children agape
As the clock tower chimes and tumbles,
The steeples on Marion Street roar like dragons,
And still the smoke keeps rising, the cotton,
Soft and terrible, breathing its hot curse
Across the sinking skyline. *Lux lucet*
En tenebris. I teach our son the old words,
Wonder what he will see in these sparks
Next year, in twenty years, in all the *falos*
I pray he and I will be blessed to burn
Together, what will be refracted even
In the flames of my own passing? Will
He see my adopted city, his birthright, burning,
Or, as I do, a feast of mountains ringed with light
Of conscience, the faithful raised again in song
One cold night each year? What unruly fires
Will burn in him? What knowledge carry
To his heart? *Descend descend*
Et baptisez nous de feu. Descend descend...
He hurls a fistful of damp magnolia leaves
Onto the small flame before I can stop him,
And we watch smoke ease like steam
around what looks just now like wet

Brown hands cupped to sacrament.
Fire fire fire! he keens as I try
To explain, when in a sudden burst
Of red curls, the leaves catch and begin
To rise to the night, sowing our portioned
Sky with embers.

SCOURGE

By Susan Levi Wallach

Think how fire leads to fire. Forty scourges with
a burning bush—one for every night of Noah's flood.
God's way, some say. A burst of flame to ruck a forehead,

leave an R for runaway, compass rose of redemption.
A hailstorm of fire and brimstone to butterfly a soul.
Some hauled by a rough-spun dress or shirt, runnelled,
neck

roped with stones that glimmered like sprat beneath the
river's rush
when the brand was not enough. That R, now for restitution.
You might say that fire is justice, finally come to pass.

ABOUT THE LITERARY ARTISTS

Al Black is the author of *I Only Left for Tea: Poems,* published in 2014 by Muddy Ford Press, as well as the founder of Mind Gravy and several other poetry and performing art collectives in Columbia, SC.

Cynthia Boiter is the editor of *Jasper Magazine* and the author of *Buttered Biscuits*, co-author of *Red Social*, editor of *The Limelight, volume 1*, and co-editor of *A Sense of the Midlands and Fall Lines, a literary convergence.* She is a six-time winner of the SC Fiction Project, a fellow of the SC Academy of Authors, winner of the Piccolo Fiction Open, the Porter Fleming Award, and a 2014 recipient of the Elizabeth O'Neill Verner SC Governor's Award for the Arts.

Elizabeth (Betsy) Breen is a recent graduate of the University of South Carolina's MFA program. Her poetry has appeared in Redivider, *Jabberwock Review, Waccamaw, Revolution House, undefined, Raleigh Review,* and *Jasper Magazine,* among others. She teaches English literature at Hammond in Columbia, SC.

Jonathan Butler›s poems, essays, and interviews have appeared or are forthcoming in *Yemassee, Jasper, Fall Lines, The Frank Martin Review*, and elsewhere. He participated most recently in the *Columbia Broadside Project*.

Debra A. Daniel, author of the novel, *Woman Commits Suicide in Dishwasher*, & poetry chapbooks, *The Downward Turn of August* & *As Is*, was twice named SC Arts Commission Poetry Fellow. She's won the Guy Owen Prize, awards from the Poetry Society of SC, Piccolo Fiction, and SC Fiction Project. Work has appeared in: *The Los Angeles Review, Smokelong, Kakalak, Emrys, Pequin, Inkwell, Southern Poetry Review, Tar River*, & *The Poetry Society of SC Yearbook*.

William Garland teaches English and Creative Writing at Montverde Academy in Montverde, FL. He is a graduate of MFA program in creative writing from the University of South Carolina. His work appears in *HOOT, The Dr. T.J. Eckleburg Review, Revolution House, The Dead Mule School of Southern Literature, Real South Magazine, Jasper Magazine* and other literary journals and anthologies.

Rachel Haynie writes frequently about art – for *Jasper, Columbia Living Magazine and Blue Fish Digest* – and history. The City of Columbia and Richland One selected the USC graduate's youth biography *First, You Explore: The Story of the Young Charles Townes,* from USC Press, for Together We Can Read 2015. For more mature readers *Charles H. Townes and a Beam Straight to the Stars* has just been released.

Ed Madden is an associate professor of English and director of the Women's and Gender Studies program at the University of South Carolina. He is the author of three books of poetry and the literary editor for *Jasper Magazine*. Madden has been named the inaugural Poet Laureate for the city of Columbia, SC.

James D. McCallister, a lifelong resident of the South Carolina midlands, is the author of two novels, *King's Highway* (Red Letter Press, 2007) and *Fellow Traveler* (Muddy Ford Press, 2012), as well as a variety of creative nonfiction publications. A two-time SC Fiction Project honoree as well as a Faulkner-Wisdom Competition and *Saturday Evening Post* short story finalist, McCallister adjuncts in creative writing at Midlands Technical College.

Ray McManus is the author of four books of poetry: *Punch.* (Hub City Press, 2014) *Red Dirt Jesus* (Marick Press, 2011), *Left Behind* (Steeping Stones Press, 2008), and *Driving through the country before you are born* (USC Press, 2007). His poetry has appeared numerous journals, most recently in *Blue Collar Review, Barely South, The Pinch, Hayden's Ferry,* and *moonShine Review*. Ray is an Associate Professor of English in the Division of Arts and Letters at University of South Carolina Sumter where he teaches creative writing, Irish literature, and Southern literature, and he is the Creative Writing Coordinator for the Tri-District Arts Consortium.

Tom Poland writes about the South, its people, land, and culture. He travels back roads looking for forgotten places, captivating people, and vestiges of bygone times, many of which appear in his columns and features. Much of that work finds its way into books. A Georgian and University of Georgia alumnus, he lives in Columbia where he writes about Georgialina, the region he calls his native land. He's written ten books and has three others underway.

Tara Powell is an associate professor of English at the University of South Carolina. She is the author of *Physical Science* (2010), a chapbook of poems, and *The Intellectual in Twentieth-Century Southern Literature* (2012), a book of literary scholarship. She co-edited *Writing in the Kitchen: Essays on Southern Literature and Foodways* (2014). Her current research projects include New South verse memoirs, Italian-Americans in Southern Appalachia, and portrayals of the South in popular literature and film.

Susan Levi Wallach was the recipient of the 2014 Thomas Wolfe Fiction Prize. Recently, her work has appeared in the *Southern California Review, American Athenaeum*, and *The Moth*. She has an MFA from Vermont College of Fine Arts and is a freelance copyeditor.

ART FROM THE ASHES CONTRIBUTING ARTISTS

Jarid Lyfe Brown

Michaela Pilar Brown

Alejandro Garcia-Lemos

Mary Bentz Gilkerson

Kara Gunter

Michael Krajewski

Whitney LeJeune

Susan Lenz

Jack McGregor

Kirkland Smith

Christian Thee

Cedric Umoja

About the Cover Artist

Cover artist Susan Lenz describes herself as the daughter of German immigrants, a wife, mother, homeowner, business woman, an avid traveler, custom picture framer, taxpayer, non-practicing Catholic, a member of a few non-profit organizations, a college graduate, a blogger, and the "servant" to an adorable cat. Yet, she is first and foremost, an artist.

Using needle and thread for self-expression, Lenz works within the scope of an overall theme and toward a final, mixed media installation. She stitches both by hand and machine, but also indulges a passion for book arts and unique, 3D found art objects. She has studied with several international artists and is regularly accepted into national juried exhibitions. Her work has been presented in solo shows across the country.

Lenz is represented by the Grovewood Gallery in Asheville, NC; Iago Gallery in Blowing Rock, NC; Earthwood Collections and Earthwood Gallery in Colorado; The American Visionary Art Museum Shop in Baltimore, MD; the Sumter Gallery of Art Shop, Sumter, SC; and at Mouse House in Columbia, SC.

ACKNOWLEDGEMENTS

The authors and editor offer sincere appreciation to the following individuals and organizations: Lee Snelgrove, Robin Waites, John Sherrer, Tom Brown, Alexia Helsley, Mark Sibley-Jones, Annie Boiter-Jolley, Caitlin Bright, One Columbia for Arts and History, the South Carolina Arts Commission, Tapp's Arts Center, Muddy Ford Press, and Historic Columbia.

ABOUT JASPER MAGAZINE

Jasper Magazine – The Word on Columbia Arts is a bi-monthly publication focusing on the Columbia, SC arts community with editors devoted to six specific disciplines: dance, theatre, music, film and the literary and visual arts. A no-profit enterprise, the Jasper editorial staff consists entirely of working artists who eschew advertorial financial support in favor of artistic integrity, relying solely on advertising dollars, reader support, and the kindness of members of the Columbia arts community at large. For more information on Jasper Magazine, please visit JasperColumbia.com

www.ingramcontent.com/pod-product-compliance
Lightning Source LLC
Chambersburg PA
CBHW061500210726
48287CB00007B/2588

* 9 7 8 1 9 4 2 0 8 1 0 1 2 *